Scotland

Turas Troimh Alba

A Photographic Journey Through Scotland

To Martha & Bill,

To help you remember your
visit to Scotland, and
wishing many happy returns.
Best Regards!
T. R. Gordon

Scotland

Turas Troimh Alba

A Photographic Journey Through Scotland

PHOTOGRAPHED & WRITTEN BY T.R. GORDON

Published by Wanderings & Wonderings

Photographs in this book are
available as enlargements suitable for framing.
For further information please contact;
Wanderings & Wonderings, 515 Woodland Hills, Carthage, Mississippi 39051

Designed by Rebecca L. Lowers
ISBN 0-9655320-1-1
Printed and bound in USA.

Dedication

This book is lovingly dedicated to
my mother and father, Gaye and Julian Gordon,
who allowed me to wander from an early age
yet always offered enough guidance
to keep me on the right path.

Acknowledgements

Producing a book is a monumental task requiring
the time, skills, and support of a large number of people.

A huge thank you to Rebecca Lowers who designed the layout
and coordinated the production on the entire project.

Thanks also to the following:
To Dan Alexander, formerly of Books Americana, Inc.
for his advice and assistance in distribution.

To my aunt and uncle, Ercel and Amadeo Galeota,
who always told me I had a talent and should write a book.

To Peter Costello, my bicycling colleague and mentor,
who reintroduced me to the joys of cycling which led to new
discoveries within Scotland and within myself.

To Linda Phillipson for typing the original manuscript,
correcting my errors, and leading me into the computer age,
with me kicking and screaming all the way.

To Shirley McGee for editing and proofreading.

And to my parents and my brother, Tony,
for all their support and for welcoming me home through
all my wanderings.

Introduction

August 31, 1983. After a long overnight flight from New York to London, I stepped off the plane in Aberdeen to be greeted by a cold blowing rain in the early morning chill. I had arrived in Scotland. Little did I know at the time, but the subtle beginnings of a love affair were hidden in those stinging raindrops half a world away from everything I was familiar with.

I was to report for duty at RAF Edzell for a two-year assignment with the U.S. Marine Corps. The former World War II Royal Air Force base is located 35 miles south of Aberdeen. Now primarily a U.S. Naval communications facility, I would be assigned to a small Marine company working closely with other U.S. military personnel from all branches of service, as well as some civilians and British military. I felt lucky in having gotten the orders to Scotland. At least the people spoke English there. Not quite the same as Mississippi English, but we were able to communicate. I could have been sent to Adak, Alaska, isolated several hundred miles midway out the Aleutian Chain, or to Misawa, Japan, with a serious language barrier or even the USS Neverdocks, floating aimlessly around the world. Yes, I was quite optimistic about my tour of duty in Scotland.

Truthfully, Scotland was not one of the faraway places I used to dream about as a child on my bicycle excursions around the neighborhood. China, maybe. Or Russia. The Amazon jungles, perhaps. Or even the moon. Orbiting around the sun. Fighting with General Washington. A child's imagination is a wonderful thing. But for some reason Scotland never entered the picture.

And yet, as I stepped off the plane, collected my gear and began the taxi ride to Edzell, there was a strange, almost eerie familiarness with the countryside and surroundings unfolding before me. I felt completely comfortable with what should have been a culture shock. Oh sure, it was a bit unnerving the first time driving on the left side of the road with a taxi driver who talked as fast as he drove, wheeling through roundabouts where six highways converge around a small circle. But there was something soothing, something delightful, even something magical, about this place. To borrow a phrase from a John Denver song, I felt like I was "coming home to a place I'd never been before!"

As I settled into my new life and new routine, moments of leisure were spent exploring the area. At first, I was without a vehicle and thus my explorations were limited to the distance I could travel by foot. But even the small village of Edzell had a fabulous castle, and pleasant walks were enjoyed along the River North Esk. I sometimes even ventured into the surrounding hills or glens, often observing deer or pheasants, or merely listening to the wind. Everywhere I traveled, I marveled at how old everything was. The stone walls and houses seemed indestructible. So much history. Experiencing it here was far superior to reading about it in a stuffy classroom.

The days swiftly passed into weeks. Eventually I bought myself a motorcycle, not always the most efficient or comfortable means of travel in Scotland, considering the weather, but certainly more advantageous than walking everywhere. After completing my work schedule, if no further military obligations were pending, I was off into the countryside. My fascination with my new home grew into a passion as I came to know more about the country, its history, its people and customs. Usually traveling to avoid the major highways, I sometimes covered very little distance in the greatest amount of time possible, using single-track roads where the combination of curves and sheep often made my average speed about 30 MPH. My theory was to take the most circuitous out-of-the-way route possible and try to return via a different route. Within a short time I knew the backroads better than some of the locals.

Eventually my tour in Scotland had to end as my Marine Corps enlistment was completed, but I always knew I'd be back. As I spent the next few winters working in ski areas, I was constantly vexed trying to figure out a means to return to my beloved adopted homeland. That opportunity came in 1989 when I got a job with a small company based in Baltimore, leading bicycle tours in the Borders region and in the Dumfries and Galloway region of Scotland.

Traveling at a bicycle's pace was even more rewarding and eye-opening than by motorcycle. Oddly enough, though I had briefly been through this area of the country during my military days, I was not that familiar with the south of Scotland and thus found new pleasures and new adventures around every turn. Our bicycling season kept us in the country from May through October, and what a fabulous way to spend the summer, with spring and autumn tacked on at the beginning and end for good measure. From lambing time to migrating geese, all we missed were the long dark days of winter. I spent several delightful summers in this fashion.

Nowadays, Scotland has become a major tourist destination. It seems more and more people are looking to discover something about their roots, their heritage. For many Americans, Canadians, Australians, and other former British Empire countries, those roots are in Scotland. The genealogy boom hasn't hurt tourism. That's for sure. Before my military assignment took me there, I was not aware that I had any Scottish ancestry. But everywhere I went in the country, people would ask me, "Aye, Gordon, how did ye come about a good Scottish name like that?" I learned that at the height of the Highland clans' powerful days, the four greatest and most populous were Campbell, MacDonald, MacKenzie, and Gordon. Maybe I really had been "coming home to a place I'd never been before."

People often ask me what it is I like so much about Scotland. What keeps drawing me back? Quite honestly, even after all these years and plenty of time to think of a clever answer, I really can't pinpoint any one thing. The conundrum seems to be irresolvable. Several things could be influential. It almost seems like time stands still somehow. That appeals to me tremendously in this fast-moving world. Life is at a slower pace, with people taking time to enjoy an afternoon cup of tea or an evening walk when the summer days linger until 11:30 P.M. There seems to be less emphasis on material possessions and extravagant consumerism, and more appreciation for the country's long, noble history while taking care of the old things and old ways in a protective manner. And as insane as it may sound, I like the Scottish weather. Contrary to popular belief, it does not rain all the time. A farmer friend of mine in the Borders said their average annual rainfall is 25 inches. That is only half what we get in Mississippi most years. Now that rainfall accumulation may come as a mist or light shower that could literally last for days. Thunderstorms are few and far between. I actually find the chilly damp days quite refreshing, even invigorating. And when the sun shines, it is heaven. Because Scotland is at a latitude about as far north as Hudson Bay or the panhandle of Alaska, the summer days are extremely long. Summer is not about heat; it's about light, an extraordinary quality of light, partly due to its angle with the sun at this northerly latitude, and also affected by the constant cloud movement and changing appearances of the landscape from the shadows. So many times my camera has not been able to capture what my eyes are seeing.

No matter if you've never been or if you've spent considerable time there, I hope you enjoy my photographic journey through Scotland. It has been an ongoing labor of love. I am forever grateful to have had the opportunity to experience it. This book is a collection of photographs and memories. The camera often led to new discoveries, meeting some intriguing characters or learning a bit of history to make the moment come alive.

By the way, the book's title is *Turas Troimh Alba*, which is Gaelic for "Journey Through Scotland." It is pronounced Tour'is to rhyme with miss. Troimh is Troy. Alba is Al'a ba, with a wee short unseen syllable thrown in. Take your time and share my journey with family and friends. As the Scots say, "Nae rush, nae bother." Slainte !

Turas Troimh Alba

A Photographic Journey Through Scotland

SHETLAND

Fair Isle

ORKNEY

WESTERN ISLES

St. Kilda

Inverness

Skye

HIGHLAND

GRAMPIAN

Aberdeen

TAYSIDE

Mull

Dundee

CENTRAL

FIFE

Edinburgh

Glasgow

LOTHIAN

Islay

STRATHCLYDE

BORDERS

DUMFRIES & GALLOWAY

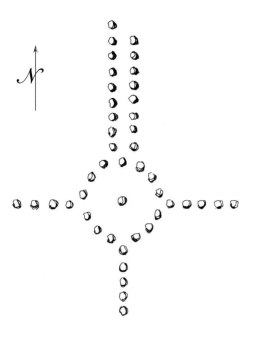

STANDING STONES OF CALLANISH
Isle Of Lewis
Outer Hebrides

On a bleak barren windswept hill in a remote corner of the Western Isles can be found one of the most remarkable sites in Scotland — the Standing Stones of Callanish. On my first trip to Lewis and first encounter with the stones, I had crested a nearby hill and the majestic apparition emerged through the mist. I wanted to get closer as quickly as possible, and yet approached with a degree of trepidation, still awe-struck. The mysterious circle of 13 stones, each 8 to 12 feet high, surrounds another taller stone of 16 feet, and the remains of what is believed to have been a burial chamber. Projecting out from the circle are rows of smaller stones, most about 5 to 7 feet high, forming the shape of what appears to be a Celtic cross, with a single row of stones in three directions and a double row of parallel stones in the fourth direction. The parallel rows of stones extend 270 feet to the north and are 27 feet apart. To the south is a single row of five stones, 91 feet long. The eastern row consists of five stones extending 75 feet, while the western row of four stones is 42 feet long. Like Stonehenge, its more famous counterpart in the south of England, the Callanish stones are still today largely an unexplainable phenomenon. Believed to be possibly 5000 years old, they may have been used for astronomical observations, religious ceremonies, or lunar/solar seasonal calculations. No one knows. Perhaps that is what makes it such an amazing place. How did these huge stones, each weighing several tons, get to this site without the advantage of modern machinery? How were they erected upright in such a significant pattern? And what is the reason for 13 stones, believed to be a superstitious number in our modern society? To these questions and many others, we will never have answers. Another smaller circle about a half mile away, within sight of the large Callanish circle, also contains 13 stones. On several visits to Callanish, I have spent the better part of the day in contemplative solitude, always with few and infrequent other curious souls arriving. It is a desolate but inspiring place, off the beaten path via a ferry trip from Skye or the mainland, but well worth the time and effort to get there. I think one needs to be something of a dreamer to fully appreciate what a monumental antiquity is here to behold.

ROSE AND ABBEY RUINS
Jedburgh
Borders Region

Shakespeare must have been in Scotland when he came up with the idea about "a rose by any other name would smell as sweet." They're everywhere. Roses have to be the most common flower in gardens large and small. Some entire cities, Aberdeen in particular, are known for their vast rose gardens.

SUNSET FROM ARTHUR'S SEAT
Edinburgh
Lothian Region

One of the capital city's most magnificent views has to be from the extinct volcano called Arthur's Seat, now surrounded by Holyrood Park. On a late summer evening, the park is crowded with cyclists, runners, walkers, and families out for a stroll. A one-way road circles The Seat, a distance of exactly five kilometers for those working out. The castle and spire of Tolbooth St. John's dominate the skyline.

CORGARFF CASTLE
Near Cockbridge
Grampian Region

Corgarff Castle, built about 1530, occupies a strategic position beside the Lecht Road. It has a long
and bloody history, from clan fighting to its last use as a base for controlling illicit whisky distilling in
the Highlands. Driving the Lecht from Cockbridge to Tomintoul, one of the highest elevation villages
in Scotland, can be a white-knuckle experience even in good weather. In winter, the Lecht is almost
always the first main road in the country to be blocked by snow.

CASTLE STALKER
Loch Linnhe
Near Port Appin
Strathclyde Region

Having never seen photos of Stalker or read anything about it, I did not fully know what to expect in my search down the west coast. My map showed roughly where it was, but sometimes my experience had been to drive right past a castle even though scanning the countryside in search of it, if it happened to be behind a copse of trees or I looked on the wrong side of the road at just the wrong instant, or my attention was distracted by sheep on the road. Such was the case with Stalker. I went right by it without seeing it, being in view only for a brief moment on the main coastal road. After traveling for several miles to the next landmark noted on the map, I knew I must have passed it and thus began backtracking and looking more carefully. When I did find it, what a dramatic situation it occupied. Standing stark and grim against the fading light of dusk, barely silhouetted against the distant hills across Loch Linnhe, I took a couple of shots but mindfully observed where I thought the early morning sun would first illumine its island setting. Photographers will go to extremes of inconvenience for just the right light. And so, a mostly restless night was spent trying to sleep in the car, in hopes of catching that first light as it hit Stalker. About 4:30 A.M. the sun's rays touched the centuries-old stone and I came away pleased with the morning's efforts. Later, when viewed under gray rainy conditions, the castle takes on a more sinister, ominous look. Stalker was built by Duncan Stuart of Appin in the reign of James IV around the year 1500.

VIEW FROM CAIRN O' MOUNT
Near Fettercairn
Grampian Region

On a fine autumn day, the hills covered with heather offer a breathtaking view. Montrose and the North Sea can easily be seen, some 15 miles away. The steep, narrow and winding road up the Cairn o' Mount is not for the timid motorist or cyclist — providing numerous white-knuckle experiences on the exciting descent. With its 20% grades and switchbacks, it was a favorite excursion from Edzell during my military tour there.

THE ROAD LESS TRAVELED
Highland Region

Without a doubt the best way to really see Scotland and feel the pulse of the countryside is by traveling the many miles of one lane roads, known locally as single-track roads. Some are no wider than your living room sofa and usually present obstacles such as sheep reluctant to move off the warm pavement on a drizzling day. All are in immaculate condition. Rarely are potholes encountered, and I have never seen an unpaved road anywhere in the country. Narrow, tiny lanes with no observable traffic and seemingly going nowhere are always in a state of good repair. Single-track roads have passing places frequently where two vehicles can get by each other. Customarily, when vehicles see each other across an open area, the one nearest the passing place will pull in, flash his headlights to signal the other to come ahead, and wait for the other to pass. It's all very civilized. Occasionally, one might unexpectedly meet a large lorry hauling livestock. In that situation, the smaller vehicle would reverse to the nearest passing place to allow the truck to squeeze through, or if one is in a daring mood, try to inch by narrowly missing the ditch or stone wall. Either way, it's great fun!

Sometimes taking these less traveled roads leads to a predicament, but more times than not, to rewards and discoveries not found on common pathways. Case in point is the high road crossing from Kishorn to Applecross in the Wester Ross area of the Highlands. For most of the 12 miles or so of the single-track road, the traveler sees no houses, no cars, no powerlines, no sign any other man has ever been here except for the tiny lane he's driving on. Warning signs at the bottom of the climb caution against 20% grades, hairpin turns, snow closures at certain times of the year and advise against inexperienced drivers attempting the route. Most hilly regions will sustain sheep if nothing else. Here, the landscape is so harsh, not even sheep are put out on the hills. As the road climbs up into the clouds, with nothing but heather and rock to accent the bleak, barren landscape, I actually imagined myself crashing through the guardrail and falling off the end of the earth.

HIGH WHEELING

While working in Scotland in 1990 leading bicycle tours, I had the privilege of participating in a fabulous event called KM 150 marking the 150th anniversary of Kirkpatrick Macmillan's invention of the pedal-driven bicycle. Macmillan is now generally credited with developing the first two-wheeled vehicle that could be balanced and propelled with the rider's feet off the ground. Before this, the bicycle of that era, known as the "hobby horse," did not have any sort of pedal system or drive mechanism and was moved by the rider sitting astride it and kicking his feet along the ground to make it go. Macmillan, a blacksmith on the estate of the Duke of Buccleuch, attached a treadle and rod to the rear wheel of the hobby horse that was, for all practical purposes, the first bicycle.

Because he lived in the seclusion of rural Scotland in the mid-19th century, Kirkpatrick Macmillan never achieved widespread recognition for his innovation. In fact, he never tried to realize any financial gain from it. His machine was more a curiosity to his neighbors, who dubbed him "Mad Pat." He was often seen pedaling along on the strange contraption through the countryside on poor roads, passing hedges and stone walls at the then unheard of speed of 8 MPH. He once traveled from Thornhill to Glasgow, a distance of 70 miles. His feat would have likely gone unnoticed if not for the unfortunate accident of his running over a young child on the sidewalk of Glasgow. Upon his appearance in court, the magistrate offered to pay his fine of five shillings in exchange for a demonstration of this odd machine.

The idea of a bicycle was not new. Various manufacturers had tinkered with many designs of two-wheeled self-propelled vehicles for a number of years. Even Leonardo da Vinci in the late 1400's had drawn sketches of what could only be described as a bicycle, 350 years before one actually appeared. Like da Vinci, Kirkpatrick Macmillan was something of a visionary, a man ahead of his time. With only his knowledge of farm equipment and how things work, and an imagination, he unknowingly revolutionized the travel of his day. Through the next several decades, the improvements in the bicycle led to a frenzied society's haste to become more mobile. No longer were people reliant on horse and buggy. A faster, more self-reliant mode of transportation was available. The bicycle had arrived.

CYCLISTS COMPARING MACHINES
Drumlanrig Castle
Dumfries and Galloway Region

ANTIQUE BICYCLES
Keir Mill
Dumfries and Galloway Region

LADS ON HIGHWHEELERS
Near Keir Mill
Dumfries and Galloway Region

THE AUTHOR ON HIS 60-INCH HIGH BICYCLE

By 1870, bicycle technology had advanced amazingly from Macmillan's wooden-wheeled, heavy steel machine. Solid rubber tires and wire spokes made for a smoother ride. However, still lacking chaindrive and gears, the general thinking at that time was "the bigger the wheel, the faster one could go." Through an evolutionary period the front wheel got larger and larger while the rear wheel got smaller, until the high bicycle was not only the preferred machine but the only bicycle available for almost 20 years. Cycling became a popular pastime and sport, offering society's first real escape into the countryside from the cities. Some saw the daring young men on their highwheelers as menaces to law and order. They were the fastest things on the road, easily outdistancing horse-drawn carriages. In addition to the dangers involved with riding an obviously unsafe machine, early cyclists also had to deal with atrocious road conditions. The problem of being thrown off the high bicycle, commonly called "taking a header", was widespread, even expected, everytime one went out for a ride. A cycling journal of 1887 advises first aid for headers, "warm water and a soft sponge should be courageously employed to extract the grit and dust from the wounded surfaces." In the early 1800's, Great Britain had smooth, well-maintained roads because everybody traveled by horse and buggy. But by the middle of the century, trains became the preferred means of transport and roads soon fell into a state of disrepair. By the time the bicycle arrived, roads were covered with potholes and generally were unsafe. Add to this, the high center of gravity of a rider on a 54-inch wheel (this being the average size) and the fact that the bicycle had a very ineffective braking system, and one had to be considered something of a daredevil or maniac to ride the machine. Still, it enjoyed an immense popularity.

The bigger the wheel, the higher rose a young man's self-esteem. In the end, of course, he was limited to the length of his legs. Because a man's average height at that time was 5'8", many aspired in vain to a 60-inch machine. Technology made machines lighter. Racing became popular. Some amazing feats were achieved by these early cyclists, such as traveling 340 miles in 24 hours.

By 1890, the pneumatic tire and chaindrive to the rear wheel had been developed leading to the safety bicycle. With two wheels the same size, it was the forerunner of today's bicycle. To distinguish it from the new safety, the highwheeler became known as the "ordinary." In Britain, where it had achieved its greatest popularity, it became known as the "penny farthing," a term now frowned upon by high bicycle enthusiasts for its derogatory connotations. At that time, the penny was a large coin and the farthing a small coin, comparative to the wheel sizes of the ordinary. Neither coin was worth very much, which is what people thought of the ordinary after the safety came along. And so, virtually overnight, the era of the high bicycle ended.

I now ride a highwheeler. People ask me why? Why do I ride such an odd inefficient bicycle? The highwheeler is an amazing machine. It has almost therapeutic qualities, both for me and the passing public. It can entice normally snarling motorists to volunteer toots on the horn, thumbs up, waves out the window, and always chuckles and shouts of glee from children who leave their games to run out for a closer inspection. The highwheeler makes people smile, something we can never have too much of. For some perhaps, it evokes thoughts of times long since passed, when life was simpler, unhurried, with qualities not found in today's society. As compared with modern bicycles, I can't go as fast. I can't comfortably go as far. I can't get up hills or down hills as easily. It's not nearly as safe. To the eye that only sees the obvious, the physical superficial things, the highwheeler is at a great disadvantage. But he has not learned how my mind works. Indeed, he may not truly know how his own mind works. The high bicycle has one distinct advantage. It is a link with the past. It is as much a time machine as it is a bicycle. It draws me closer to my affinity for old things—things of quality that have no fear of time. In addition to the aforementioned friendly reactions and joys of people seeing such a marvelous machine, this is its simple advantage. It transports me to places I could not go otherwise. Not places on the road, but of the heart.

TRAFFIC SIGN
Edzell
Tayside Region

Driving is an adventure in Great Britain. Obviously, driving on the left side of the road is the biggest adjustment. I had often wondered how the custom had started. As it was explained to me by a friend in the Borders, it stems back to medieval times. When knights were jousting, they approached each other on horseback so the lances in their right hands would be opposite each other in battle. When motor vehicles appeared, approaching each other in this manner continued. Many other factors have to be considered as well for safe driving. Road signs and driver etiquette are sometimes similar to ours with only slight changes to get accustomed to. For example, the sign here is much like our "Yield" except that it can also replace "Stop" at certain intersections, which I liked because I'm the world's worst driver in my habit of rolling through a stop sign without fully stopping. With "Give Way" that's exactly what one is supposed to do —-keep it moving if all is clear.

VIEW TO THE CHEVIOTS
Lochside
Near Yetholm
Borders Region

A typical country lane, bounded by hedges and fields, and just wide enough for a small car and bicycle to meet without either having to take to the ditch, was the usual route I took daily from our cottage during one of my summers working in the Borders. The distant hills are the Cheviots, which form a natural boundary between Scotland and England.

CORTACHY CASTLE
Cortachy
Tayside Region

I first discovered Cortachy while stationed at RAF Edzell. With a number of other Marines, we staged a 50-mile bicycle ride as a fund-raiser for Toys for Tots, with the route being several backroads from Edzell to Kirriemuir. I remember the route was most enjoyable with rolling hills and bordered by stone walls. The return trip brought a strong headwind and actually forced us to pedal downhill to avoid being brought to a standstill. Cortachy has long associations with the Ogilvie clan. The 15th-century castle is supposedly haunted by a ghostly drummer who betrayed the family and was burned to death.

EVENING LIGHT AND DRY STANE DYKES
Near Dunscore
Dumfries and Galloway Region

SHEEP ON LITTER BOX
Grey Mare's Tail
Dumfries and Galloway Region

Sheep are known for wandering just about anywhere they can conjure up in their minds to go. Sometimes fences and boundaries have no effect. They squeeze through holes seemingly too small to accommodate them. These two were encountered while I was cycling through the Yarrow Valley toward Moffat. On a high road just beyond St. Mary's Loch (the only loch in the Borders) I had paused at a rest area, enjoying the airshow being provided by the Royal Air Force. A great deal of their low-level flying is done over Scotland, due to its relatively sparsely populated areas as compared to England. The jets zoomed through the valley, unheard until they were right on top of me as they moved faster than their sound. In places where the road went along the top of the valley, I would often be looking down on the planes as they crossed the treetops in the valley below. The sheep seemed oblivious to all the activity.

WINTER GRAZING
Glen Esk
Tayside Region

15

INVERMARK CASTLE
Glen Esk
Near Edzell
Tayside Region

This roofless ruin is situated in beautiful scenery at the entrance to Glen Esk. A stronghold of the Lindsay clan, the tower was built at the beginning of the 16th century. Being only a short distance from the military base at Edzell where I was stationed, it was one of the first castles I visited. The outing to Invermark was made with several Marine buddies of mine. We were quite eager to explore the inner chambers of the antiquity, but the entrance in its present condition has no access from ground level. It is about eight feet off the ground and was formerly entered by a huge drawbridge. Not to be denied just because the entrance is up where the second floor should be, we clambered and scrambled up on each other's heads and shoulders until the ascent had been successfully completed. Perhaps inevitably, a near tragedy ensued. One of my comrades slipped and tumbled out the eight-foot high entrance, remarkably injuring only his pride and a slight sprained ankle.

DUNNOTTAR CASTLE
Stonehaven
Grampian Region

Dunnottar Castle, occupying the summit of a cliff-bound rock overlooking the North Sea, was practically unassailable throughout its long history. The top of the rock is flat, forming a platform of 3 1/2 acres. On every side the sheer cliffs drop to the sea 160 feet below. A site of such obvious advantage could not have been overlooked in turbulent times. The buildings that form the most prominent features of the castle still existing were built in 1394. One of the best known legends of Scotland is associated with Dunnottar. During the wars with England, Oliver Cromwell's armies were steadily tightening their hold upon Scotland. By May of 1652 the only place still flying the royal flag was Dunnottar. The Crown jewels - crown, scepter and sword - had been brought to the castle for safekeeping. After Cromwell's bombardment and siege began, the Regalia were daringly smuggled out and lowered over the walls on the seaward side to a waiting boat below. The minister's wife from nearby Kinneff Church helped transport the jewels down the coast a few miles where they were hidden under the church pulpit. After an eight month siege, Dunnottar surrendered. But the disappointed English never found the Crown jewels. They are on display today in Edinburgh Castle. Now it's the Scots who have the upper hand. They charge the English (and everybody else) four pounds sterling to see the Crown jewels.

THE ROUND-UP
Near Keir Mill
Dumfries and Galloway Region

ICE CREAM TWINS
Princes Street Gardens
Edinburgh
Lothian Region

On previous cycling trips past Drumlanrig Castle, I had noticed a very cheerful-looking cottage with flower boxes and a fence with various children's toys always lying about. But never had I seen any people there. A most amusing sign across the road warned of free range children, much like the caution signs in remote areas where livestock are not fenced in but have open range to graze. I thought it a clever and ingenious way to get motorists to slow down, even though this tiny lane couldn't have an overwhelming amount of traffic. One day as I was passing, I saw a lady out in the yard. As I got off my bicycle to talk to her, two adorable wee little girls came around from behind the cottage. I asked if they were the "free range children" mentioned on the sign. The lady answered, "They most certainly are." I asked if I could take their photo beside the sign. The mother agreed and the children galloped over on stick horses. As can be seen, the younger one had a very short attention span and was all set to exit, but big sister took charge of the situation and held her in tow until I got focused. Their sweaters and red cheeks are evidence of a cool summer day.

I observed two wee girls enjoying ice cream on a fine summer day in the Gardens. It was hot for Scotland - 80°- and the twins' pace of eating was a bit slower than the melting capacity of the sunshine. I asked their mother if I could take a photo. She gave her approval, and apparently had not noticed until my interest in the children that their arms, legs, and dresses were dripping with the flavor of the day.

OAP Crossing
Near Aberfoyle
Central Region

Senior citizens are referred to as Old Age Pensioners, or usually just OAPs.

Awaiting The Summer Crowds
Princes Street Gardens
Edinburgh
Lothian Region

QUEEN VICTORIA
Jedburgh
Borders Region

KING GEORGE VI
RULED 1936 - 1952
Near Glenfinnan
Highland Region

KING GEORGE V, RULED 1910 - 1936
Dryburgh
Borders Region

ROYAL MAIL LETTERBOXES

Who would have ever thought mailboxes interesting enough to make a case study? After learning a little about them, I was intrigued by their histories. Each is elegantly made bearing the reigning monarch's initials at the time of its installation. My favorites are those from Queen Victoria's era. Most have a fancy intertwined V R for Victoria Regina (Regina is Latin for queen. A male ruler would have been denoted by an R also, Rex being Latin for king). If the letterbox had been installed early in Victoria's reign, it could be 150 years old today. With untold layers of the Royal Mail trademark red paint, they look as good as new. The letterbox I'm particularly keen to find, if it exists, is one from the short reign of Edward VIII. He was king for less than a year, so there may be no letterboxes, or they could have been removed since he abdicated the throne to marry an American divorcee, the scandal of the century at that time.

Her Majesty's Royal Mail is known for delivery to the far reaches of the countryside. For example, in the U.S. on rural routes, at the end of a long dirt road may be 20 mailboxes for all the residents who live down that road. They have to come to the end of the road to collect their mail. Not so with the Royal Mail carrier in his cheerful red van. If a single cottage is situated all alone at the end of a single-track lane several miles from the main road, the mail is delivered to the door, as is the case with all residences. Small town post offices are known to deliver such items as groceries and medicine to remote addresses along with their mail.

QUEEN VICTORIA, RULED 1837 - 1901
Traquair
Borders Region

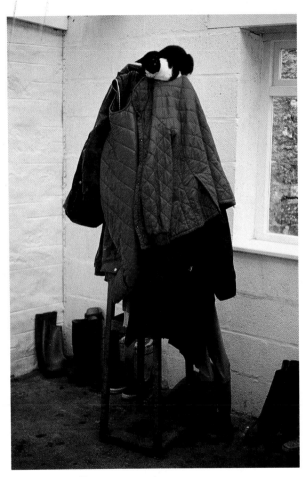

CAT ON COAT RACK
Hobsburn House
Bonchester Bridge
Borders Region

No doubt seeking refuge from the two playful Labrador retrievers in the house, this cat found a quiet spot out of reach in the boot room.

BED AND BREAKFAST
Doune
Central Region

In my opinion, the best way to travel in Britain is to use accommodations in bed and breakfast establishments. The name is exactly what it implies; people open their homes to guests for an overnight stay and breakfast the next morning. It's inexpensive, cheerful, comfortable, and a great way to meet the locals. B&B's are readily found in every village, town or city throughout the country. Often in rural areas, farmhouses offer B&B accommodations. Most hosts are extremely helpful and knowledgeable in assisting one with planning activities in the area to facilitate the optimum use of leisure time.

CURIOUS COWS
Near Haugh of Urr
Dumfries and Galloway Region

I had dismounted my bicycle and paused for a drink of water when I noticed several cows lumbering in my direction. At first they stopped a few yards away, but gradually one by one inched closer until they were all peering over the stone wall. Not quite knowing what their purpose or intentions were in being there, but feeling very jolly myself after a good morning's ride, I sort of made mooing sounds which made them look even more curiously. Finally, my brief respite over, I got on the bike and started pedaling away. Oddly enough, the cows responded by breaking into a trot and then a fast run as my momentum increased. I only outdistanced them when another wall stopped them at the end of their pasture.

Traveling by bicycle, I often observed small details that would have gone undetected at automobile speed. Milk delivered to the door was one custom still alive and well, thriving and common even in Edinburgh, a city of 500,000. Empties are placed in a designated spot, and in the pre-dawn chill the friendly neighborhood milkman makes his rounds to exchange fresh milk for the empties. Older people, now called senior citizens except in Scotland where they are OAPs (Old Age Pensioners) often recount from their childhood how the milk would freeze on winter mornings and push the foil cap right off the bottle. It was also something of a treat to get the first glass from the bottle, after the rich cream had risen to the top. This was back when people could eat what they wanted before the cholesterol thing came along. I have seen milk at the end of a country lane with no house in site, still waiting to be picked up at mid-day. Apparently, there is no concern for spoilage owing to the cool pleasant temperatures even in summer. In small towns, where the milk was delivered before the grocer opened, it was simply stacked at the front door and early morning shoppers would leave their money lying on top of the crate.

MILK BOTTLES ON
DOORSTEP
Near Kelso
Borders Region

MILK IN DELIVERY BOX
Near Tushielaw
Borders Region

MILK AND NEWSPAPER
Farm on the Bowmont Water
Near Yetholm
Borders Region

THE GLENFIDDICH DISTILLERY
Dufftown
Grampian Region

One of the country's most famous exports is Scotch whisky, or in the old Scots Gaelic "uisge beatha"— water of life. To connoisseurs of fine whiskies, nothing compares to the single malt Scotch. The heart of Scotland's whisky industry lies here in the Spey Valley. The names of single malts also denote the geographical region they are produced in — Glenfiddich, Glenlivet, Tamdhu, Glenmorangie. This potent spirit is derived from malted barley, usually smoked over a peat fire, natural Highland spring water and yeast. Each single malt has its own distinctive flavor and color, from years of maturation in oak casks. Walk into any pub and you will surely arouse a lively debate in asking what the local favorite whisky is, for it's all a matter of personal preference and rarely agreed upon. An old saying concerning Dufftown, long established as the center of whisky-making, is "Rome was built on seven hills; Dufftown stands on seven stills."

Incidentally, the barrels pictured here are empty. Those containing the Scotch are kept in a closely monitored, controlled environment under lock and key. The distillery manager has one key and Her Majesty's exciseman has another key. Both are required to gain entry.

FORTH RAILWAY BRIDGE
North Queensferry
Fife Region

The Forth Railway Bridge celebrated its centennial a few years ago, having been built in 1890. Its massive humped girders are a sharp contrast to the graceful road bridge a short distance away, opened in 1964. Until that time, ferries had crossed the Firth of Forth between South and North Queensferry for 900 years.

SWAN AND CYGNETS
Edzell
Tayside Region

The RAF installation in Edzell had a small lake that had become known as Loch Wee. Here lived a family of swans. The adult pair were highly protective of the young, constantly hissing and snapping at passersby. They roamed freely around the base, leaving a messy trail wherever they went, if you know what I mean. But to see them take flight, with their huge wings furiously beating the air until finally they were up and off the water, was poetry in motion.

News of The World from The Sunday Times
Pittenweem
Fife Region

All is quiet around Pittenweem harbor on this Sunday afternoon; no fishermen about, no lorries being loaded, no fishmongers shopping the market for the catch of the day. Just a couple reading the paper and enjoying the warm spring sunshine.

FISHING HARBOR
Crail
Fife Region

TOOLS OF THE FISHERMAN
Stonehaven Harbor
Grampian Region

A North Sea storm left this early dusting of snow on nets and ropes. The town was still asleep as I had gotten out early for a Sunday morning walk around the harbor. Without having heard a weather forecast, I was taken by surprise with the white ground cover. Not that the Scottish meteorologists are any more reliable than our own American weathermen. In fact, they may be even more vague. The typical forecast usually reads something like this: Starting dull, becoming changeable to fresh by afternoon. That leaves a lot to the imagination.

WEE GIRL AND PUPPY
Pittenweem
Fife Region

THE BIRDMAN OF PRINCES STREET GARDENS
Edinburgh
Lothian Region

On a chilly autumn afternoon, as the days are getting shorter and the shadows longer, I was taking a stroll through the Gardens and happened upon this old gentleman who was surrounded by birds. He obviously came to this same bench frequently and had quite a relationship with his feathered friends, who eagerly responded to his whistles and ate right out of his hand. He would sometimes have to scold and reprimand the larger pigeons to make room for the wee sparrows.

Pittenweem is normally a busy fishing village, but on a Sunday afternoon there are quiet times in the harbor. Sandbags in the doorway of this cottage would seem to indicate recent high tides with a scattering of seaweed on the landing.

OLD GENTLEMEN
Kelso
Borders Region

On my frequent trips into Kelso during summers of leading bicycle tours, I often chatted with this group I had affectionately dubbed "The Old Boys Club." They were usually hanging around the town square enjoying the sunshine on the cobblestones, reading a newspaper, discussing the market price of lambs or generally just watching the world go by. I never knew if their rendezvous was prearranged by some sort of daily tryst, or if they just happened to be in the square by coincidence.

LOBSTER TRAPS AND NETS
Crail
Fife Region

Crail is just one of many picturesque fishing villages on the coast of Fife, often called the East Neuk. A small fleet still operates from here, but the lobster traps, nets, gabled houses and red-tiled roofs nowadays attract more artists and photographers than fishermen. I learned while poking around the harbor that lobster traps, called creels, are scrubbed after each use and dried in the sun and wind. Only small, inexperienced lobsters will enter a smelly creel.

They shall grow not old as we that are left grow old.
Age shall not weary them nor the years condemn. At the going down of
the sun and in the morning, we will remember them.

—FROM THE WAR MEMORIAL, EDINBURGH CASTLE.

ROYAL SCOTS GREYS MEMORIAL
Princes Street Gardens
Edinburgh
Lothian Region

A handsome equestrian statue over-looks Princes Street Gardens, a tribute to the Royal Scots Greys regiment. I had seen it many times in passing down Edinburgh's main thoroughfare, but never had it looked so splendid as on this winter evening silhouetted against a brilliant sunset. Scotland has always had a long and proud military tradition, as evidenced by countless war memorials in cities and villages throughout the country.

EDINBURGH MILITARY TATTOO
Edinburgh
Lothian Region

An event not to be missed in Scotland in August is the Edinburgh Military Tattoo, an extravaganza of music and pageantry with the castle esplanade as the stage and the floodlit walls of the centuries-old castle as the backdrop. The Tattoo is held nightly except Sundays for about three weeks. The program changes each year, but certainly the highlight for most people is the annual appearance of the massed bands of Scottish regiments with their pipes and drums. I've seen the Tattoo a number of times and the spectacle never fails to send chills all over my body, as the pipes and drums emerge from the castle gate on the esplanade. First, the sound seems faint and small against the large, dark Edinburgh night, but as they continue to cross the bridge four abreast and fan out as they reach the esplanade, the volume grows into a huge crescendo when one realizes there are now perhaps 100 pipes and drums. A most impressive sight and sound! Each year there are groups from other countries, presenting a truly international gathering. Each evening, the performance closes with all the spotlights off, the castle dark, and a lone piper high on the ramparts playing a haunting lament. Then the night sky bursts alive with fireworks.

The word "Tattoo" comes from a Dutch custom of the 17th-century. British forces stationed in the Low Countries were summoned back to their quarters at night by fifes and drums of their regiments marching through the streets. Innkeepers and pub owners would then "doe den tap toe" or turn off the taps. From this humble means of enforcing opening hours, a Tattoo became a ceremonial performance of military music by massed bands.

KILCHURN CASTLE
Loch Awe
Strathclyde Region

The ruins of Kilchurn, a former Campbell property, occupy a picturesque setting in Loch Awe. The castle is sited on a rocky promontory which is sometimes an island and sometimes connected to the mainland by a marshy peninsula, but was evidently cut off entirely from the land when the castle was built in the 15th century.

CESSFORD CASTLE
Near Morebattle
Borders Region

The ruins of Cessford, a once massive castle between Kelso and Jedburgh, presents a sharp contrast to the gentle farmland surrounding it. The castle was stronghold of the Kers, ancestors of the Duke of Roxburgh and an influential Border family. Cessford was built in the 14th century. It ceased to be a dwelling house in 1650, but was later used as a prison. The Kers were known as being a predominately left-handed family. Consequently, many castles formerly associated with the family have their spiral stairways twisting opposite from most. This was so the upper levels could be more advantageously defended during attacks with swords, giving the left-handed residents more arm room for fighting.

The bright yellow crop, seen growing profusely throughout Britain, is oil seed rape. Its primary use is for making canola oil for cooking.

Cessford remains for me something of a mysterious ongoing study. Often overlooked on maps and seldom found in books, I have been able to gather only scant information on it, even after spending a year and a half in the Borders. One local historian related to me that it was at one time the third strongest castle in all of Scotland, after Edinburgh and Stirling. Its ruins prove that it was at another period in time a formidable fortress of considerable size. Unlike many fine castles in the country that are cared for by the National Trust for Scotland or Historic Buildings and Monuments under the Secretary of State, Cessford is maintained by no one. It sits alone on a hill in a fenced pasture, with no admission fees and no custodian, no entrance gate and no pebbled walkway. Its companions are the wind and rain, birds and cattle, and the rare occasional visitor like me, curious to explore and eager to see what tales can be conjured up in the imagination. Perhaps that's what intrigues me the most.

DARKENING CLOUDS
Morebattle
Borders Region

These are the skies that made for interesting experiences while I was outdoors all summer on bicycle tours. Showers could pop up anytime unexpected, but often by the time one could get his raingear out, the shower had passed and it was sunny again. After several encounters, through experience, I would know which clouds and which skies justified bothering getting suited for rain. Would this cloud produce an all-day washout or simply a "turnip green shower"?

Trying to get a straight answer from a local concerning the weather could be as irritating as a persistent skin rash. I honestly believe it's a national conspiracy, a sworn secrecy not to discuss the weather. Ask anybody what the weather is going to do, the answer is something like, "Don't know" or "Haven't heard" or "Och, I dinna ken." (I do not know.)

GORSE HILLSIDE
Near Shawhead
Dumfries and Galloway Region

One fine spring day in May, I was cycling and came upon a very aromatic fragrance. The hill was covered with a shrubby bush with yellow flowers, and a delightful smell that I could only compare with suntan lotion or some sort of tropical beverage. It was a combination of coconut and pineapple, an absolutely exhilarating aroma. I stopped to refresh my senses of smell and sight, as the lovely yellow flowers were alive with insects, and when a little breeze came through, the fragrance in the air was intoxicating. I later learned the plant is called gorse. I wish I could put a "scratch and sniff" spot right here, because you'd surely love it.

THISTLE - THE FLOWER OF SCOTLAND
Near Cauldhame
Central Region

How did the thistle become so closely associated with Scotland, even considered a national emblem? According to legend, in a field at Luncarty near Perth, Scots king Kenneth MacAlpin escaped disaster on a dark night when an invader yelled after stepping on a thistle and warned of a surprise Danish attack.

EILEAN DONAN CASTLE
Dornie
Highland Region

Eilean Donan Castle is undoubtedly the most photographed castle in Scotland. It can be found on numerous postcards, calendars, books, whisky bottles, shortbread tins and even a few movies. It is superbly situated on a rocky promontory at the meeting point of three lochs — Loch Long, Loch Duich, and Loch Alsh. Today, it entices the visitor with a romantic, almost dream-like quality in such a splendid setting. But in days gone by, it was a fortress of solid stone and formidable defenses. It had to be, with Norse and Danish marauders raiding along these coasts. Later, it served as a stronghold during clan wars in the Highlands. The name Eilean Donan is an old Gaelic form of "island of Donan" and was named for a religious hermit who lived on the island in the early 7th century.

Eilean Donan has long been a stronghold of the MacRae clan. It was partially destroyed in 1719 when three English ships sailed into Loch Alsh and bombarded the castle. The ruins remained neglected for 200 years, falling into a state of disrepair until a restoration effort by descendants of the MacRaes rebuilt it in the early 1900's. A story behind the restoration is quite unique. One of the MacRae descendants had a dream that revealed the castle's appearance before it was destroyed. There were believed to be no authoritative sketches or blueprints in existence. Later, after the castle had been rebuilt, some old papers were found at Edinburgh Castle showing Eilean Donan before it had been destroyed. It was exactly as the dream had revealed.

URQUHART CASTLE
Loch Ness
Near Drumnadrochit
Highland Region

The impressive ruins of Urquhart Castle show evidence of its importance through the years, constantly being sacked and rebuilt in war and peace. It is probable that there was a castle here as early as 1200 A.D. Urquhart's setting, on the shores of Loch Ness, adds to its legendary status, for it is often in the vicinity of the castle that sightings of the so-called Loch Ness Monster have been reported. The loch is a mile wide and 25 miles long, up to 1000 feet deep, icy cold, dark and mysterious. With an equal number of believers as skeptics, the controversy surrounding the existence of "Nessie" continues as it has for centuries. One of St. Columba's monks reputedly narrowly escaped becoming a snack for the monster some 1300 years ago. My own theory concerning a monster in Loch Ness is this. The monk who narrowly escaped so many years ago was part of an abbey at the south end of the loch, near the present-day site of Fort Augustus. These facts we do know. What is not widely known is that these monks, who are recorded to have seen an unexplainable creature in the murky depths, were also the first to learn the science of distilling whisky. Could their new beverage have contributed to certain hallucinations?

SUNSET ON LOCH FYNE
Strathclyde Region

Though this photo was taken on a lonely road on Lewis, it is representative of the entire country. I have constantly been intrigued by the most remote settings imaginable, stark cold landscapes with no houses around, and there sits the trademark bright red British Telecom phone booth, often accompanied by a handy bright red letterbox for posting Her Majesty's Royal Mail. I suppose it's a good idea. Not that the urge often strikes me, out in the middle of nowhere, to call somebody or stop and write a postcard, but if those urges did arise, the facilities are available and ready to use. I also noticed there are no street names in rural parts of Lewis. For instance, 27 Callanish denotes a certain house in the village of Callanish and 42 Arnol is a particular cottage in the village of Arnol. No street is given, merely a house number. Also confusing is the possibility that #14 might be next door to #38. Houses are numbered in sequence of when the properties were purchased, not necessarily consecutively by location.

ALONG THE BOWMONT WATER
Near Yetholm
Borders Region

A shepherd's office, though not very spacious, does come with excellent views.

POSTCARD VENDOR
Edinburgh
Lothian Region

This old gentleman was one of my regular encounters while I was in the city. I think he made a decent living with his wares in the summer when the tourist traffic is so tremendous. In fact, I always suspected he left Edinburgh and her damp dark winter days for a leisurely life on the beach in the Bahamas, only to reappear the next summer and proclaim "Harry's Back."

LAB WATCHING TRAFFIC
Edinburgh
Lothian Region

While strolling down the Royal Mile, I passed under this window with a black Labrador Retriever curiously watching the comings and goings along the street. He appeared cozily ensconced in his quarters, with a pillow under his legs for comfort. I believe he was an old dog, judging by the graying around his muzzle and whiskers, and likely he had spent many days in the past in this same perch. A few people who obviously passed his way daily stopped to pet him and he seemed very friendly. At one point, his master, also aging and gray around the whiskers, assumed an identical position alongside the dog, sipping on a cup of tea and greeting neighbors as they passed.

GLENFINNAN MONUMENT
Loch Shiel
Highland Region

In 1745, a young prince named Charles Edward Stuart gained enough support to start an uprising against the British government. His objective: to regain the throne of Britain for the Stuarts. Through a complicated series of events, a previous Stuart king had been forced into exile. From an early age, Charles had an obsession that it was his destiny to reclaim the throne. Glenfinnan is the spot where he landed with two French ships and a handful of Highlanders rallied around him. The rising, known as "The '45", gained momentum and Charles enjoyed several important early victories against the English. But in the end, nine months later, his forces were slaughtered at Culloden near Inverness. The prince escaped, wandered as a fugitive with a huge bounty on his head for several months, and eventually returned to France. Though nearly captured several times, he was never betrayed by the common people who endured tremendous hardships to protect him. He is now known to history as Bonnie Prince Charlie. His story is one worth reading - both romantic and tragic - and had many long-term effects on the Highland way of life. The monument at Glenfinnan is not a tribute to him, but rather to the general character of all Highlanders who were left after Culloden to pay the prince's debts by persecution or death and attempts to destroy their culture, beliefs and very existence.

RED CASTLE
Lunan Bay
Tayside Region

Very little remains of this 12th-century castle on a cliff overlooking the lovely beach at Lunan Bay. Its name likely derives from the reddish sandstone it is constructed from. It was another of my favorite excursions during my military days at RAF Edzell, being only 15 miles from the base and easily accessible by bicycle or motorcycle. Because of its usually cool summers, Scotland could by no means be considered a bikini paradise, and the beach at Lunan was always uncrowded. On bright days, the water glistened in the sun, sparkling radiantly like a million diamonds dancing on the surface as if some benevolent giant had scattered them with a mighty toss. Indeed, I enjoyed many fine contemplative moments on the sands at Lunan Bay in the shadow of Red Castle. Naturally, you can modify the dream to suit your own taste.

SCOTS GUARDS
World Pipe Band Championships
Glasgow
Strathclyde Region

The colorful kilts and plaids of the Scots Guards provide a photo opportunity as they make final preparations before competing. The tartan is Royal Stuart. The four stripes on the lower right sleeve identify the pipe major. The elaborately adorned dirk also functions as utensils for eating, with a small knife and fork contained in the scabbard. It costs well over $1,000 to outfit each piper in a Scottish regiment.

BAGPIPE SHOP
Edinburgh
Lothian Region

Several years ago I wandered into a bagpipe shop in Edinburgh, in an alley just off the Royal Mile. There I met an older gentleman named Bert Rowan, who is an accomplished piper, instructor and pipemaker. The shelves of his workshop are stocked with varying lengths of African blackwood, the heart of all good quality bagpipes. A set of Highland bagpipes contains 14 pieces of wood, each carefully bored and lathed to produce the proper tonal qualities. It takes Bert 8 or 9 days to make a set of pipes. Nowadays, he calls himself retired, working from 10:30 to 4:30 or whenever he feels like it. I still stop in to see him and exchange pleasantries whenever I'm in Edinburgh. He seems almost as intrigued by my Southern colloquialisms as I am about his pipemaking.

CURIOUS LAD
Royal Gathering at Braemar
Braemar
Highland Region

Usually when bagpipe bands perform, the crowds gather in, but always keep their distance. The sound can be quite overpowering near the instruments. I noticed this little guy making his way closer for a better view, totally oblivious to all the activity around him. He was definitely focused on this new spectacle, seeming to wonder about these men wearing what looked like his mother's dress and making all sorts of noise from a bag stuck under their arms. He seemed to be enjoying himself thoroughly.

"Sounds
which might jar the nerves of a Londoner or Parisian,
bring back to the Highlander his lofty mountain, wild lake and
the deeds of his fathers of the glen."

SIR WALTER SCOTT, SPEAKING IN REFERENCE TO THE MUSIC OF THE BAGPIPE.

MASSED PIPE BANDS
Royal Gathering at Braemar
Braemar
Highland Region

Certainly one of the most thrilling sights and sounds for any visitor to Scotland is the parade of the massed pipes and drums always seen at highland games, military tattoos and other ceremonial events. The impressive and stirring sound of several hundred bagpipes, coupled with a colorful mix of tartans and plaids, will long be remembered.

SUMMER FIELDS
Near Hownam
Borders Region

CRAIGIEVAR CASTLE
Near Alford
Grampian Region

Completed in 1626 after 16 years of construction, Craigievar Castle resembles something out of a fairy tale with its turrets, chimney stacks and gables. It was the seat of the Forbes clan, with family treasures and magnificent ceilings of beautiful plasterwork inside. This area of the Gordon District in the Grampian Region is so thickly populated with fine castles open to the public that the local tourist board actually promotes a "Castle Trail" with detailed brochures and information for visiting the properties.

A most interesting legend concerning Craigievar relates to a long-standing feud between the neighboring clans of Gordon and Forbes, who apparently were not the best of friends. During one particular night, a surprise visit by one of those Gordon fellows found him climbing to the upstairs window. An ensuing skirmish found the Forbes lad gaining the upper hand. To avoid the disgrace of being killed by a Forbes, the Gordon chap leapt out the window. Whether he survived or not depends on which family's descendants are telling the story.

PLOWING PATTERNS AND STONE WALLS
Near Moniaive
Dumfries and Galloway Region

Sometimes when I'm bicycling along I seem to be doing lots of writing in my head, trying to organize my thoughts and make observations of what I'm experiencing. Then when I get to a convenient stopping place or have my writing materials accessible, the mental notes are transcribed onto paper. The paths through the fields where tractor tires move caught my eye as interesting patterns, but by the time I got to the point where I could write it down, the thoughts had escaped me. I remember getting sidetracked when I saw a car from France, obviously a family on holiday. Europeans don't go on vacation; they take a holiday. Anyway, this car had a different license plate and a sticker on the back with an "F" on it, so I knew it was from France. I got to wondering if the French eat French-style green beans, or French fries, or French vanilla ice cream, and that messed up my ideas about the plowing patterns.

ARDCLACH BELL TOWER
Near Nairn
Highland Region

Quite by accident, I sort of stumbled upon this interesting old bell tower and its even more interesting system of security. After seeing the sign for the tower and finding the key hanging there for anybody to use, I thought it worth the visit. An old church built in 1626 is on low ground with hills rising all around. In early years, that caused a problem, because the sound of the church bell carried only a short distance. The bell served a dual role. Obviously it summoned parishioners to Sunday service, but also was the warning that cattle thieves or sheep reivers had been seen. So the separate present bell tower was built on the hillside above the church.

EDZELL CASTLE
Edzell
Tayside Region

My military assignment in Scotland meant Edzell was my home for almost 2 1/2 years. Consequently, the castle was the first I visited in the country and one I would return to frequently. A shortcut footpath through the woods and across the River North Esk made a delightful 2-mile walk to the castle, and if enough time was mine for leisure I would spend the better part of a day walking through the garden or climbing the circular stairway to the upper parapets for a grand view of the countryside. Edzell Castle, dating from the early 15th century, was the stronghold of the Lindsays of Glenesk. The garden, added in 1604, is one of the finest examples of Renaissance landscaping in Scotland. The elegance of the early castle cannot be imagined today from the ruinous condition, but it was the most magnificent residence in this region and for luxury had no equal. For the sumptuous banquets frequently held in the great hall, the kitchen had a fireplace with the enormous dimensions of 23 feet long and 10 feet high. The Lindsays were well known as sympathetic lords to the poor and freely dispensed hospitality at the castle. Oxen were roasted whole in the giant fireplace, and accompanying dishes served in the same huge portions. Each day, after the family had dined, the lady and daughters of the castle served food to the parish poor. The stone benches in the courtyard, where they gathered for this generosity, still remain.

HIGHLAND CATTLE
Near Kilmuir
Isle of Skye

Soon after I arrived in Scotland, I was surprised by my first view of Highland cattle. The shaggy, long-horned breed are especially suited to the cold, windy weather that Highland winters can bring. They remind me of a cross between a musk ox and a Texas longhorn. I have been told they are generally a docile animal, not nearly as fierce as they appear.

BALES OF HAY
Near Hownam
Borders Region

This symmetrical pattern caught my eye while cycling past. If a farmer does not have adequate barn space, the large bales are wrapped in plastic and left outside during the winter.

WILDFLOWERS
Lochside
Near Yetholm
Borders Region

Sometimes I feel the entire country is one huge flower garden, inconspicuously connected by roads, towns, farmlands and hills. Flowers are everywhere, in all varieties imaginable and a kaleidoscope of colors. From tiny cottages to multi-acre parks, gardens are always immaculately groomed and cared for. Many villages, towns and cities boast of several years of consecutive wins in a national competition called "Britain in Bloom" which recognizes the best-kept public areas for general appearance and attractiveness.

HAY DRYING FOR BALING
Near Stobo
Borders Region

This was one of my favorite cycling areas, along the Manor Water south of Peebles. Several of the highest hills in the Borders are round about. Absolutely glorious countryside. Nearby is the small village of Stobo, home of a fancy health spa in an old castle. As I furiously pedaled along, with perspiration dripping off my chin and giving my heart and legs a good workout, I imagined what society ladies might be doing in the spa. Never did I venture inside the rather imposing-looking gates to catch a glimpse of the social elite. Perhaps their faces were plastered with that avocado unction that looks like guacamole, while enjoying a mud bath and sipping mineral water.

THE EILDON HILLS
Near Melrose
Borders Region

Famous through both Border folklore and history, the Eildon Hills' three rounded summits are visible from most corners of the region. The ancient Romans had established camps and lookout posts atop Trimontium, "the three mountains", nearly 2000 years ago in this most northerly settlement of the Roman Empire. Legend has it that one Thomas Learmont, also known as Thomas the Rhymer, lived in the nearby village of Earlston in the 13th century. Here he supposedly met the Queen of Elfland, who enticed him to follow her into the kingdom of the wee folks. He had to stay for seven years. If he spoke during that time, he could never return home. His silence was rewarded by being empowered with the gift of prophesy. He returned home and was for many years known for his wisdom and profound observations. Another legend concerns Merlin the magician of King Arthur fame. Merlin is said to be buried inside the Eildon Hills. No matter what fact or fiction surrounds the Eildons, a hike to the top rewards the adventurous with marvelous views of the Borders. For the even more serious athlete, a hill race to the summits of the three hills and back down is a highlight of the summer festival in Melrose.

WATERFALL ON EAST SIDE OF LOCH AWE

Near Portinnisherrich
Strathclyde Region

SUNDIAL AT LINTON KIRK

The lichen-covered sundial on a corner
of the church bears the inscription - My
days are like a shadow that passeth.

LINTON KIRK
Near Yetholm
Borders Region

This small church at Linton is over 850 years old. A plaque inside lists the
previous parish ministers, beginning in the year 1127. It is a lovely setting
on a hill with grand views of the surrounding Roxburghshire. Upon arriving, I found the door locked, but the key was in the lock. Visitors are wel-
come. An interesting cemetery with some very old gravestones is worth
exploring.

RAM, EWES AND LAMBS
Near Moffat
Dumfries and Galloway Region

The importance of sheep to the Scottish economy cannot be overemphasized. From the Borders to the Highlands, from the East Neuk to the Western Isles, sheep are to be found in pastures and on hillside, as far as the eye can see. The fields come alive each spring when the lambs are born. From wobbly, unsure legs, they very quickly emerge into frisky bundles of energy. I spent many blissful moments in the warm spring sunshine watching lambs playing like hyperactive children. Sometimes one would jump straight up in the air and dart about as if pursued by an imaginary friend. They're almost like children, running and playing with several little friends. One may be seen on a mound of dirt, butting heads with the others as "king of the mountain."

Moffat is a major center of the sheep industry. In contrast to most towns, the main street has a statue, not of a famous soldier or statesman, but of a ram.

SHEPHERD AND BORDER COLLIE PUP
Near Moffat
Dumfries and Galloway Region

This handy means of transport carries shepherd and dog to the high ground. The pup is likely going out into the pasture for some intense training, to capitalize on his natural instincts for herding. Border collies are truly amazing dogs. No shepherd could do his job without one, or several, depending on the size of his flock.

SERIOUS BUSINESS
Glen Esk
Tayside Region

The warning sign says it all. Because newborn and young lambs are so vulnerable to many dangers, the shepherd must take all precautions.

LOCH ARD
Central Region

RAINBOW
Near Hownam
Borders Region

I like rainbows. I think most dreamers do. There seem to be lots of songs about rainbows and what's on the other side. With the frequent drizzling weather and sunny intervals, Scotland has its fair share of rainbows. Sometimes my progress is impeded by the appearance of a rainbow, or even a double rainbow. Not that they present a major obstacle to my passing, but I always have to stop and watch and wonder until the last faint hint of color has faded into oblivion. I have often seen, just yards away, where a rainbow touches the ground, but never has it produced the fabled pot of gold. Still, it gives me inspiration in other ways. Too often we see a thing of beauty, and instead of stopping to appreciate it, we try to overanalyze it or make it seem complicated. We get obsessed looking for the pot of gold at the end of the rainbow, and yet, when we finally find it, we realize we had it all the time. Next time you see a rainbow, stop and enjoy it. It's a gift. That moment must be savored right then, for soon it will be gone forever.

FRANK THE CROOKMAKER
Ettrickbridge
Borders Region

On my cycling rounds I frequently stopped to visit Frank, a fellow who earns his livelihood making shepherds' crooks. I never knew his last name; just "Frank." I had seen shepherds working in the fields and always using a crook, whether to grab a sheep by the leg or neck to catch it, or as a support while walking on hills and uneven ground. It appeared to be a most useful and necessary tool. In my visits with Frank, I learned that most shepherds have two or more crooks. A standard basic rough design with no frills would be used for everyday work around the farm, but a fancier model with intricate, ornate carvings and decoration would be for formal outings, such as going to church or social calls.

MOVING SHEEP TO MARKET
Isle of Harris
Outer Hebrides

FREE RANGE GRAZING
Near Broughton
Borders Region

THE MOLE CATCHER
Hermitage Castle
Near Newcastleton
Borders Region

I met Walter Blakey on a chilly March afternoon with snow still lingering in the hills around Hermitage. He's a mole catcher, sometimes with 60 traps set at the same time, and remembers where each one is. He described to me and demonstrated how his handmade traps work better than commercially produced ones. Walter Blakey, who started his career at age 5, has caught a lot of moles in his lifetime. Now he does it in his spare time, mainly as a public service to local farmers and landowners. He charges no fees for his services. One nearby farm had recently been eradicated of 170 moles in nine days.

MOLE CARCASS DISPLAY
Near Lilliesleaf
Borders Region

I distinctly remember the scent before the sight of the mole catcher's grisly display. While bicycling along a lovely country lane, the unmistakable odor of a dead animal permeated the soft summer aromas of blooming wildflowers and hedgerows. As I rounded a bend in the road, I was taken aback by the sight and smell of decaying mole carcasses hanging on the top strand of a barbed wire fence, as uniformly and neatly displayed as a row of guards at Buckingham Palace. I thought the whole scene quite odd, even grotesque, but my curiosity was aroused enough to look around briefly. Not that I stayed to enjoy a picnic or linger for long, but I realized this was a most effective advertisement for the person who lived in the nearby cottage, a man hired to kill moles and obviously very successful at his task. I counted 74 victims on this day. On several return journeys along this same route later in the summer, I noted the display had grown larger.

PEAT DRYING
Isle of Lewis
Outer Hebrides

CUTTING PEAT
Isle of Skye
Inner Hebrides

On the barren moors of the islands, where trees are rare or nonexistent, peat is a major source of fuel for heating. The marshy conditions are ideal for the decay of heather and other plant matter, which through many years forms peat bogs. Usually in May the peat cutting begins for the following winter's fuel. It takes a month to cut enough, about 15,000 peats, for a family of four. It is soggy and saturated with moisture, so gets stacked to allow sun and wind to dry it through the summer. It is then brought to the house and stacked for the winter. Often the stack of peat is as large as the cottage.

BELTED GALLOWAY COW
Near Haugh of Urr
Dumfries and Galloway Region

Unusual markings make the Belted Galloway easily identifiable, with a white strip around the belly. Belties, as they are commonly called, are found in all parts of the country but originated in the Galloway area. I remember the first time I saw one, I thought it had some sort of white cloth or covering tied around its midsection. Then when I noticed every cow in the pasture looked exactly the same, I realized the white belt was peculiar to the breed.

SMAILHOLM TOWER
Smailholm
Borders Region

Sir Walter Scott spent many of his boyhood summers around Smailholm. The tower is situated on Sandyknowe Farm, which was the property of the poet's paternal grandfather. Smailholm is a typical medieval keep, a type of fortification built on a simple square design of three stories and with walls of great thickness.

I recall fondly many fine picnics on Smailholm's windy rocky knoll, often being interrupted by cows grazing around the tower. But perhaps my most pleasant memories are of a gradual declining hill when departing; so gradual it hardly seemed a hill at all, but with furious pedaling on a bicycle, speeds of 45 MPH were easily attainable.

ROSE AND FENCE
Near Edzell
Tayside Region

RURAL COTTAGE
Glencoe
Highland Region

Glencoe - the glen of weeping - was made famous by a notorious massacre in February 1692. A company of soldiers, under a Campbell commander, massacred 40 MacDonalds who had been their hosts for a fortnight. The Campbells rose at 5 A.M. and in the middle of a snowstorm began the slaughter, murdering their hosts, burning their houses, and leaving the women and children to die in the blizzard. Glencoe is still a wild and lonely place, especially in winter. Its name is synonymous with the rugged harsh life of the early Highlanders, and the often brutal rivalries between neighboring clans.

ROSE AND SNOW
Stonehaven
Grampian Region

An early dusting of snow crept in unexpectedly off the North Sea in November and startled the still-blooming roses. I had left a bed and breakfast where I was staying, for a wee walkabout through town and down to the harbor, with its squawking gulls seemingly confused by the white cover. Upon my return to the B&B, I noticed the roses.

KELSO
Borders Region

Kelso is certainly one of the most handsome and charming of all the Border towns, with a cobblestone town-square and flowers in abundance. The town is dominated by the ruins of Kelso Abbey. It suffered the same fate at the hands of the English as its counterparts at Melrose, Jedburgh and Dryburgh. 800 years ago, it was the largest and richest of the four great Border abbeys, but today is in a more ruinous condition than the others. The River Tweed flows through the town, with a lovely walk along its banks to Floors Castle.

TANTALLON CASTLE & BASS ROCK
Near North Berwick
Lothian Region

Tantallon was built by the Douglas family about 1350. They were one of the most powerful clans in the Borders. The large and once strong fortress was protected by a massive 12-foot thick, 50-foot high wall on one side. The waters of the Firth of Forth and height of the cliff were its defense on the other three sides. The castle was once described by geologist Hugh Miller as "three sides of rock-like wall and one side of wall-like rock."

Nearly two miles off shore is Bass Rock, a mile in circumference and 420 feet high. On the top are seven acres of grass. A huge cavern, 30 feet high and 500 feet long, passes through the rock. A ruined castle is situated on the Bass, as is a lighthouse built in 1902. Earliest stories of the rock date from the late 6th century, when it was supposedly used as a religious refuge by a St. Baldred. Nowadays the only inhabitants are rabbits, a few sheep grazing on the grassy top, and numerous bird species.

When I arrived at Tantallon on this March afternoon, Bass Rock was not even visible. Though I knew it was out there, a thick North Sea fog provided a cloak of cover. I patiently waited, pondering the possibility of the fog lifting. The pungent aroma of slurry being spread on the fields at nearby Auldhame Farm did not exactly complement my lunch of cheese and baps. But as photography has taught me, patience is a virtue, and finally The Bass appeared.

PUBLIC FACILITIES AT KIRK YETHOLM
Borders Region

Public toilets would not normally be deemed noteworthy to most travelers, but in Scotland every town and village has immaculately clean facilities for the comfort of anyone "taken short" and requiring a visit to the WC. This sign I thought most interesting because of its very precise distance.

FIRE FLAPS
Isle of Skye
Inner Hebrides

With directions for their use in Gaelic, I wasn't sure what these were, but after studying the situation for a moment decided they must be an emergency measure for putting out wildfires. I saw them frequently in remote parts of the Highlands and Islands where a fire could spread quickly if not noticed by a traveler. So the necessary tools for extinguishing the flames were conveniently nearby.

GAELIC ROAD SIGNS
Isle of Lewis
Outer Hebrides

The ancient language of Gaelic is still spoken by about 80,000 people in Scotland, primarily in the Western Isles and in some remote areas of the Highlands. In fact, Gaelic is now being taught to school children in the hopes that it will be preserved in future generations. In a few instances, primarily with elderly people, Gaelic is their only language. Today most Gaelic speakers also speak English, but as recently as a century ago, Gaelic was spoken by 250,000 people. Of this number, nearly 20% knew no other language. The renewed interest in maintaining the language has included such measures as erecting signs in Gaelic, which can be very confusing if not for the road numbers. One may not know which town he's going toward, but will at least know which road he takes to get there.

GAELIC - ENGLISH ROAD SIGNS
Isle of Skye
Inner Hebrides

LOCH AILORT
Near Roshven
Highland Region

EVER FEEL LIKE YOU'RE TRAVELING IN CIRCLES?
2 1/2 miles (either direction) from Coull
Grampian Region

PORTREE HARBOR
Isle of Skye
Inner Hebrides

Skye is Scotland's most visited island with something for everyone - picturesque villages, rugged coastlines, mountains, dramatic scenery. For hundreds of years, the main crossing from the mainland to the island was a short ferry ride from Kyle of Lochalsh to Kyleakin. Then in 1995, after years of debate and amid a storm of controversy, a bridge opened and the ferry ceased operating. For me and untold thousands of visitors, part of the romance and intrigue of visiting the island was the ferry trip, going "over the sea to Skye."

One of my memorable crossings involved a coat hanger, of all things. While waiting in the queue with several other cars, all parked bumper to bumper to maximize the space, the ferry approached. Suddenly the car in front of me could not move. Its owner and passengers panicked upon realizing they had locked their keys inside the car. Since all the cars were parked so close together, nobody in the queue could move. I anticipated this could develop into quite an ugly scene and knew immediate action was required. I saw myself as one of the principal players in this little drama, and thus sought out a nearby car that had clothes hanging in the back. I retrieved a coat hanger and went to work. During my years in the grocery business, I became quite adept at opening locked car doors for little ladies who had left their keys inside. Without giving away any of my trade secrets, shall I just say the car was unlocked to the delight of the other ferry passengers, and we all boarded on schedule.

BEN NEVIS
Viewed from Corpach
Highland Region

Ben Nevis, here covered with snow and partially shrouded in clouds, is the highest peak in Britain at 4,406 feet. In May, 1985, I decided to climb Ben Nevis. I wanted to play the bagpipe from the top of Britain's highest mountain. Some of my friends thought I had a slight irregularity of intellect. Some still do. Anyway, with my pipes in my backpack on a warm sunny morning, the ascent began. I was perspiring profusely within a short time. As I went higher, the temperature dropped and soon I was trekking through snow. Luckily, I had packed warm clothes also. Snow was now 6 inches deep, still lingering from winter storms. Finally, the summit was reached, the pipes were played and the tremendous view was savored. I began the descent, which logically went much faster than the ascent. I was exhausted, but satisfied with the day's efforts upon reaching the bottom.

JEDBURGH ABBEY
Jedburgh
Borders Region

Located on the busy A68 highway, one of the primary north-south arteries for traffic between England and Scotland, Jedburgh is a historic town. Just twelve miles north of the border, it was often caught in the skirmishes that raged between the two countries for centuries. It was also visited by many famous travelers: Bonnie Prince Charlie in 1745, Robert Burns in 1787, and Sir Walter Scott, who, in 1793, made his first courtroom appearance as a lawyer. But the most notable visitor was Mary, Queen of Scots. She spent some time here in 1566. The town is best known nowadays for its splendid ruined abbey. It was founded in 1138 by Augustinian canons from northern France. Two miles north of Jedburgh is the old course of Dere Street, a Roman road built 1900 years ago.

HARVEST APPROACHES
Near Fintry
Central Region

HARRIS TWEED
Isle of Lewis
Outer Hebrides

Though the map clearly states two names, Harris and Lewis, it is actually one island. Nowhere on a map or on the geography of the land are the two separated. The northern larger part of the island is Lewis; the smaller south is Harris. Equally odd, Harris tweed is made on Lewis. The world famous material is still woven in individual cottages, then collected and transported to the mill. Tradition and skills are passed down through the generations.

DAVID MCGREGOR
Selkirk
Borders Region

David Mcgregor is a master craftsman at Selkirk Glass, a company that specializes in hand-crafted paperweights. He is a very personable fellow, a characteristic obviously recognized by his employer, since he usually works in the area where visitors are allowed to see production firsthand. He carefully explains each step of the paperweight-making process. It takes David about 20 minutes to make a paperweight, which must cool down gradually in a kiln for 24 hours to avoid cracking. He is a highly skilled craftsman and a jolly nice fellow as well.

HAIRPIN TURN
Isle of Skye
Inner Hebrides

Skye's rugged beauty attracts visitors with a sense of the outdoors; climbing and hillwalking are favorites. The landscape is dominated by the Cuillin Hills, with a feeling that one is never far from a coastline. Skye's irregular coast means no place is more than five miles from the sea.

DRY STANE DYKE REPAIR

Near Selkirk, Borders Region

While cycling over the long and grueling Ashkirk Hill between Ettrickbridge and Lilliesleaf, I stopped on top to talk to a man repairing a stone wall. His name was Jock Davidson and his is an important skill in a country with literally thousands of miles of stone walls, or as they are known locally - dry stane dykes. The stanes (old Scots word for stones) are put together without any type of mortar, thus they are called "dry". I imagined the work to be something like a huge jigsaw puzzle, with each stone having a particular place to fit according to its size and shape. It could be a tiring and lonely occupation, working secluded on a distant hillside, but must also be highly rewarding and satisfying to be able to look back down a wall previously in a dilapidated state and see it finely aligned and perfectly shaped. The reward must also be in working with one's hands, creating something useful that lasts, breathing the fresh country air and troubled only by the thoughts brought to the hill that day. Many of the old master craftsmen are retiring now or dying, and someone must be trained to continue their legacy. Dyking courses are now available for younger lads wanting to learn the trade.

WILLIAM MACDOUGALL

Years later, I wanted to find out more about dyking and stopped at the police station in Selkirk, hoping they could direct me to a local person skilled in the trade. An extremely congenial and helpful officer named Murray Macdougall directed me. "You need to talk to my father. He's one of the best dykers in the Borders. He'll either be on the hill or in his favorite pub just now." Then he showed me in a very old dusty book of police records where his father had been arrested for poaching fish 50 years earlier. "Aye, but he's a fine dyker!"

William Macdougall, who is 71 years old, started dyking in 1947. He worked a six-month apprenticeship with no pay, bicycling everyday up the Ettrick Valley to the work site. He related to me some very interesting facts and stories of his years as a dyker. He can repair six yards a day, if working with good stone and no major prob-

lems. The average height for a wall is 4 feet 6 inches with the width 2 feet at the bottom and tapering to 14 inches at the top. There is a ton of stone in each yard of wall. Some of the stone originally came from nearby fields as they were cleared, but most of it was quarried and hauled in. Walls need repair, periodically, from several factors. The foundation stones could shift with soggy ground, since the wall also goes several inches into a foundation that has been dug out of the ground. Livestock can knock stones out of place, such as cattle scratching their backs or heads, or sheep trying to jump over. If one stone gets knocked out, a sheep will try to go over. Naturally, others follow, with each knocking more stones out of place. The main purpose for using stone walls instead of wire is the protection they provide for the livestock, offering shelter from wind or blowing snow. Bill told me of a severe winter in 1963, when snow covered the dykes for 14 weeks. Hay had to be flown in via helicopter for the sheep. Some of the sheep, huddled behind dykes, got buried by blowing snow drifts. Six weeks later they were dug out, having been kept alive by drinking melting snow and breathing through air pockets.

And so, dry stane dykers, something of a visage from the past, are still at work in modern-day Scotland. With the simple tools of pick and shovel for shaping the foundation, a hammer for chipping or shaping stones as minimally as possible,

JOCK DAVIDSON

and two strings for aligning and leveling, he carries on the age-old art. I jokingly asked how often the walls needed repair, "every 100 years or so?" The consensus reply was, "Not that often." Most of the dykes were built 200 to 300 years ago.

Bill Macdougall still passes by the first dyke he built almost 50 years ago. It's still "in good nick." No need for repair for, maybe, another 150 years or so. I thoughtfully considered the possibility of leaving something so beautiful and so strong for posterity, placing my hands on the cold stones and remembering the hands that had carefully put them there so many years ago.

HUNTLY CASTLE
Huntly
Grampian Region

Though not the most impressive ruins or the most dramatic setting of the many castles I've visited in Scotland, Huntly is nonetheless one of the most important to me personally, because it was the ancient stronghold of the Gordons. During the era of the clan system in the Highlands, the Gordons were the largest and most powerful in the northeast of Scotland. Huntly was the center of the Gordon lands, and even today the town has numerous streets, businesses and schools bearing the name of Gordon.

GRAVESTONE AT MELROSE ABBEY
Melrose
Borders Region

It is not my intention to present myself as a person who dwells on the macabre, but I thoroughly enjoy exploring old cemeteries. I try to read the dates and epitaphs, wondering what the person was like. In my visits to many ancient burial sites throughout the country, I often see a skull and crossbones on markers with dates usually unreadable due to their age and decay. I had often pondered over the meaning of these symbols, since my only association with them previously had been on flags of pirate ships in childhood reading or bottles of poisonous substances. After talking to several friends and getting no reasonable explanation, finally I learned from the curator at Melrose Abbey the significance. With a heavy Scottish brogue, he said the skull and crossbones were an "elly clistin" symbol of death. I embarrassingly asked him to repeat himself three times before realizing he was saying "early Christian" symbol of death. This particular marker also has an interesting hourglass lying on its side. Perhaps the sands of mortality slowly trickling into eternity? Thought-provoking epitaphs are common and lead me to reflective contemplation. Two of my favorites were both found in a tiny cemetery in Kilfinan, Strathclyde Region. One of them featured an hourglass with the inscription: My glass is run, and yours is running. Be wise in time, your day is coming. The other profoundly read: I was once as thou art now, I am now as thou must be, Therefore prepare to follow me.

MELROSE ABBEY
Melrose
Borders Region

Melrose Abbey, together with those at Jedburgh, Dryburgh and Kelso, comprise the four great Border abbeys. Melrose was founded in 1136 and was the first Cistercian monastery in Scotland. Like the other Border abbeys, their position so near the English boundary was tragically their downfall with repeated attacks through the centuries of warfare. Being very innovative and successful in farming and raising sheep, the early monks brought great prosperity to the community. Their life was not an easy one, rising at 4 A.M. and not retiring until 10 P.M. with a day filled with manual labor, prayer and religious duties. I tried to imagine what it would have been like to have been here 800 years ago; waking up on a cold dark rainy Scottish winter morning, walking through the damp cold stone corridors by candlelight to milk the cows or tend the sheep. Certainly it was not a life for any but the truly dedicated, the pure at heart.

CAIRN OF REMEMBRANCE
Grampian Region

Edinburgh, Scotland's handsome capital city, is home to some 500,000 residents. It offers an exciting mix of history and old world charm in addition to cultural events and modern convenience. In the summer, particularly, the city is extremely busy, bustling with visitors as it hosts an international festival.

An excellent view of Edinburgh is afforded by climbing the narrow, winding staircase leading to the top of the Sir Walter Scott Monument. The monument overlooks Princes Street, the city's main thoroughfare, which is widely acclaimed as one of the loveliest avenues in all of Europe, and also the only main street in a European city with shops on one side only. On the other side of Princes Street is a ravine containing the railway station and the beautiful Princes Street Gardens, filled with flowers and trees, for relaxation in the city center.

PRINCES STREET GARDENS
Edinburgh
Lothian Region

Most of Edinburgh's historic buildings are in the area adjacent to the castle and leading down to the Palace of Holyroodhouse, the royal family's official residence while in Scotland. This centuries-old street is called the Royal Mile.

Narrow lanes, called wynds and closes, lead off the Royal Mile, twisting through courtyards and between shops. In medieval times, when protection from invaders was within the walls of the city and in the castle, townspeople thought of the end of the world as being just outside the city gates. The close leading off the Royal Mile at that point came to be known as the World's End.

BAIRNS IN PRAMS
Beauly
Highland Region

I was naturally curious the first time I encountered strollers with children in them outside a shop. It was cold and raining, but the toddlers seemed very content with their plastic bubbles pulled down around them, cozily ensconced with blankets and teddy bears. Some shops, because their aisles are narrow and floor space is limited, do not allow prams. It is a common practice for mothers to leave children unattended on the sidewalk outside the store. Only once have I seen a child crying in its pram, and that was an infant whose pacifier had fallen out. I put it back in her mouth and she was quiet and happy again.

GREYFRIARS BOBBY'S STATUE
Edinburgh
Lothian Region

Greyfriars Bobby was a Skye terrier that lived in Edinburgh in the mid-19th century. He was apparently named after Greyfriars Church, which was in the area of town where he lived. His master, John Grey, died in 1858 when Bobby was two years old. For the next 14 years, until his death, the little terrier stayed on or near his master's grave. His devotion captured the hearts of Edinburgh residents, who adopted him and brought him food and water everyday. Bobby died on January 14, 1872, aged 16. Finally, his long vigil ended; he was buried near his master in Greyfriars Churchyard. Today the graves are visited by countless admirers from around the world, still inspired by the little dog's tremendous loyalty.

HERALDIC UNICORN
Edinburgh
Lothian Region

This panel, originally over the entrance to a gatehouse, bears the royal arms of King James V. It is full of symbolisms representing Scotland, including the lion rampant, thistles, crowns and the St. Andrew's cross.

DEACON BRODIE'S TAVERN
435 Lawnmarket, The Royal Mile
Edinburgh
Lothian Region

A favorite watering hole along the Royal Mile in Edinburgh is a pub called Deacon Brodie's Tavern. The attractive decor with etched glass windows and flower boxes, coupled with the cobblestone streets outside, provides a cozy respite while one is walking through the city. The amiable ambiance belies a darker historical connection between the pub's name and a questionable character from Edinburgh's past. William Brodie lived in the city in the 18th century, and was Deacon of Wrights and Masons of Edinburgh. He was a respected citizen and businessman by day, but unknown to his friends and colleagues, was a thief and burglar by night. It was this dual personality that served as a basis for Robert Louis Stevenson's novel, *The Strange Case of Dr. Jekyll and Mr. Hyde.* In an ironic twist of fate, Deacon Brodie had designed a new gallows for Edinburgh's executions and later was the first to be hanged on it.

EDINBURGH CASTLE
Edinburgh
Lothian Region

Edinburgh's dominant landmark has to be its castle, perched on its rock high above the city with a commanding view of the surrounding countryside. Parts of the castle date back to the 11th century. It is still used as a military barracks and garrison. It is the most visited national monument in Scotland and second in Great Britain only to the Tower of London. The castle is visible from all around the city, and makes for a most impressive skyline.

An accurate time check while in Edinburgh is the 1 o'clock cannon fired from the castle. Ships in the Firth of Forth use it to synchronize their clocks. An amusing story was told by one of the tour guides at the castle, who are all retired military men and very entertaining as well as knowledgeable. Why not shoot the cannon at 12 o'clock? That seems more logical since many places mark the noon hour by some means. Well, the Scots are known as being thrifty, even bordering on tightfisted, and it's much cheaper to fire the cannon once than twelve times.

CHARLIE DOUGLAS
Laurencekirk
Grampian Region

Charlie Douglas has been my friend longer than anybody else I know in Scotland. He was the first person I met upon my arrival at RAF Edzell in 1983 while assigned there with the Marine Corps. Charlie is custodian of the Marine barracks. His work is outstanding, his manners impeccable, his attitude and outlook positively admirable. In his 20 years at the base, as a Ministry of Defense employee, he has twice been recognized as Civilian of the Year for the superb performance he gives, being selected over several hundred other civilians. His accomplishments are exceptional for anyone, but consider this fact. Charlie cannot hear or speak. Yet somehow, he was always knowledgeable of everything happening on the base, whether visiting VIPs or a surprise inspection. He is also one of the finest soccer referees in the area, and has been known to eject a player for using obscene language. They forget Charlie reads lips.

EQUINE PEDICURE
Bonchester Bridge
Borders Region

The Borders Region is horse country. Going back hundreds of years when horses were the primary mode of transportation, and Borders townspeople periodically rode into the hills to patrol their common grazing areas from raiding Englishmen, the tradition of horsemanship runs deep. This fellow I met in Bonchester goes to area farms putting shoes on horses, filing hooves or whatever needs to be done....sort of a roving blacksmith.

TAKE THE HIGH ROAD
Isle of Skye
Inner Hebrides

An old song in Scotland goes — "Ye'll take the high road and I'll take the low road, and I'll be in Scotland afore ye." This comes from an old Celtic belief that when a man dies in a foreign land, his spirit will return to the place of his birth by an underground fairy pathway — the low road. The song tells of two soldiers imprisoned in England. One was to be released and would have to trudge many days and long weary miles before reaching Scotland again. The other was to be executed, but his spirit in its supernatural journey on "the low road", would be home long before his comrade taking "the high road."

THATCHED COTTAGE AND A CROFTER'S LIFE
Near Mingarry
Highland Region

A croft is, loosely defined, a small farm worked by a tenant, usually just a cottage with a few outbuildings and meager numbers of livestock.

PHEASANT
Near Killearn
Central Region

WINTER SUNSET AND MOONRISE
Near Edzell
Tayside Region

THE FREELAND-COOK FAMILY
Cliftoncote Farm, Near Yetholm, Borders Region

I first met Paul, Angela, Allistair, Daniel and Murray in the early summer of 1992. The bicycle tour company I was working for was headquartered at their farm, where we rented a cottage and workshop. We spent six months there, working in close proximity to them as they went about their busy lives operating a large sheep farm in a lovely area of the Borders. They are a wonderful family and always made us feel at home. Though always extremely busy, they gladly interrupted any chore to offer us help or information to make our tours run smoothly.

Cliftoncote is an old established farmstead, with parts of the main house dating back to the 16th century. There are also three cottages and a number of barns and stables. The primary income is from sheep. There are about 1000 yowes (ewes) and 20 tups (rams) with approximately 1500 lambs born each spring. The lambs are sold for meat in autumn. Wool is not a major source of income, being more of a by-product. The sheep still have to be clipped in summer but the wool is not worth very much in the breeds they raise. Incidentally, it's called clipping in Scotland and shearing in England. The farm also has about 60 cattle, four horses, chickens, ducks, goats, and of course border collies. The job of raising sheep on a large acreage with a good deal of hilly pasture would be impossible without several good herding dogs. They are amazing.

I spent many happy times with Paul and Angela and their three fine sons. Over an afternoon cup of tea we might discuss dry stane dyking, or which field needed to be plowed next, or the proper way to mount a highwheel bicycle. But usually, naturally the conversation turned to sheep. Lambing, inoculations, marking for identification, clipping, more inoculations, the entire year seemed to be occupied with attending to the needs of the sheep. I learned so much about sheep, I almost feel I could run a sheep farm myself. Well, not quite, but I am sure I know more about sheep than I'll ever need. For example, if a lamb is born and appears to be puny or slow in getting going, it can be put in the warming drawer of the oven and given a wee nip of whisky, which usually helps it to perk up. If a lamb dies, the skin can be removed and tied to an orphan lamb, usually resulting in the mother of the dead lamb accepting the orphan as her own after smelling her own scent on the skin.

One more story about sheep and then we'll move along. I found this very interesting and unusual. Sometimes a sheep will get upside down on its back and can't get up, whether from scratching itself, rolling the wrong way or however. Its legs are quite spindly in proportion to the body weight, particularly when the fleece has a full year's growth just prior to clipping. A sheep can actually die if unable to upright itself, from pressure of the rumen against other organs and suffocation. I learned this early on in my cycling career in the Borders, and have actually seen and rescued several sheep by dashing into a field and rolling them over. If they were not down very long, they would get right up and run away. However, if they had been down for some time and gotten weak from struggling, they might stand up a bit wobbly and take a few minutes to regain their strength and senses. I asked Paul about this and if there was a word for it. He said, "We call it couped, but I'm not sure what they would call it in the States, or even in other parts of Scotland, for that matter." So I referred to Mr. Webster's dictionary and, sure enough, there it is. Coup: overturn, upset.

I've returned to Cliftoncote several times since my wonderful summer there, and my affection and admiration for the Freeland-Cooks continue to grow.

JES, WITH PAUL DRIVING

Daniel returns after a day on the tractor. A large portion of the arable land at Cliftoncote is used for growing hay, turnips, and various grains to feed the livestock.

Paul does inoculations prior to lambing, putting extra antibiotics into the ewes' bloodstream and milk to produce strong healthy lambs.

Angela attracts an attentive audience, eager for their daily rations. The different color markings on each ewe's fleece identify which farm each belongs to, which ram is the father of her lamb, and when the lambing will occur.

Angela feeds the girls as Tan keeps a watchful eye.

AUNTIE B
Cliftoncote Farm
Near Yetholm
Borders Region

One of the most charming and delightful people I've met anywhere is a dear, little lady called Auntie B. She lives in one of the cottages at Cliftoncote Farm, spending her days lovingly caring for a number of animals that might be classified as a menagerie. Horses, cattle, sheep, dogs, cats, ducks, chickens, guinea pigs and at different times of the year, of course, all their babies. She is a special person with animals. I've never directly asked Auntie B many personal questions, like her name, age or how she arrived at Cliftoncote with Paul and Angela. Incidentally, she's not their aunt, either. They just call her Auntie B like everyone else. She did tell me once that she was over 75 years old, but was born "after the First War." A friend told me her name is Hermione Bartholomew. None of that matters. What's important is the spirit with which she goes about her daily chores, the sparkle in her eyes, and the friendship we've developed since I first met her.

I enjoy helping Auntie B with her work whenever I'm back visiting at Cliftoncote. It gives us a chance to talk, and she is a fine conversationalist. She is well-read and knowledgeable about most anything - from the Kentucky Derby, to the most recent woes of the Royal Family, to the Tour de France, to the weather.

In her younger years, she was a breeder of racehorses. Her cottage walls are covered with photographs of champion horses she raised and trained. Probably, her love of animals stems from this past vocation. She treats them royally, feeding them in the morning, letting them out to pasture on warm days, letting them stay in their stables on cool days. She has names for most of them, even the 50 or 60 sheep.

The first time I met Auntie B, I was with Peter Costello, my 6'5" cycling colleague. This diminutive lady is stepping across the courtyard with a huge bale of hay on her back, with straw sticking in her hair and clinging to her jumper. Peter offers his assistance, but she says, "That's lovely, but I can manage. I've been doing this a long time." There are people in this world who, after having been with them, make one come away feeling better about life and the whole grand scheme of things. Auntie B is one of those people.

Grizelda, the big draft horse, has a gentle disposition and fondness for apples and carrots. We often gave her treats enroute to the bicycle workshop. According to Auntie B, Grizelda weighs "about 20 hundredweight, but she's small compared to Clydesdales."

The most difficult, hectic time of the year is when the sheep are lambing. Because they do sometimes have difficulty in birthing, a vigil must be maintained around the clock, particularly with those expecting twins or triplets, which has been predetermined by ultrasound scans. Here Murray does his stint on the midnight shift in the lambing shed.

Newborns spend time with their mothers, learning each other by sound and smell so that when they are put out on the hillside after a few days, they will be less likely to get separated. A lamb lost from its mother could become a fatality.

Milly is a lamb that "lost her mummy" and gets her bottle every morning. She is always at Auntie B's heels, following her like a puppy and waiting for her next meal.

Murray returns a lamb to its mother. The lamb was playing with its new pals and tried to suckle from another ewe across the pen. Ewes will butt lambs away that are not theirs, determined by sniffing for her own's smell.

Stella, on the roof, is a real barnyard cat; a bit nervous around people, not that easy to get close enough to touch, not exactly wild but not housebroken either, skinny and wiry with a stalking hunter's look about her. She was without a doubt one of the finest mousers I've ever seen, seldom without a rodent in her mouth.

JEAN
Cliftoncote Farm
Near Yetholm
Borders Region

Jean was my favorite border collie at Cliftoncote. She was the mother of one of their present working dogs, all amazing animals who control the movements of 1000 ewes and their 1500 lambs. Jean was very old, now stricken with arthritis and failing senses, and not wanting to associate much with the other dogs. She had spent a full working life on the hills of Cliftoncote, a hard life from what I could observe, and was now living out her last years in reluctant retirement. But when she heard the whistles for the other dogs to go to work, she somehow managed to hobble painfully out to the hillside. For a while she seemed to forget or at least ignore her arthritis, jumping over fences and seeming to try to teach the young dogs a few of the skills she had so long ago mastered. And her eyes would sparkle with a hint of her former glory.

Murray surveys the surrounding hills to ensure no sheep were missed by the dogs making their sweep to bring them in for the evening feeding.

Allistair and Murray round up stragglers on horseback to facilitate covering the far reaches of the hill pastures as quickly as possible.

Linny

Moss

Tan

The Dogs of Cliftoncote Farm

No sheep farm could operate without several good border collies. Cliftoncote is no exception. The Freeland-Cook family has four working dogs. Each is unique in size, disposition, temperament and abilities. One may be more aggressive, another may be faster, another may work better alone. Each can be used in particular instances to better advantage using its specific strong points. For example, a number of ewes needed to be brought down off a high pasture for inoculations a fortnight prior to lambing. At that advanced stage of pregnancy, they don't need to be hurried or run very fast. Tan is an extremely fast and aggressive dog, so she was not ideal for that situation. Jes and Moss were chosen for the job, because they are more even tempered with the slow sheep and move only as they are commanded, which is what was needed for that task.

All border collies have a natural inborn instinct for herding. However, they do require training. Some obviously are faster learners than others. They must learn commands for controlling large flocks, either whistles or voice commands being the norm. I have watched dogs for hours on end and am still constantly amazed at their ability, stamina and tenacity. It is not uncommon to see them airborne over a 5-foot-high stone wall, slithering through a small hole in a fence, or even running across the backs of a tightly-packed flock of sheep. One afternoon I watched Angela bringing a large flock of sheep down off a high pasture, working with Tan. She was at the bottom of the hill and Tan was working the sheep. From a quarter of a mile away, Angela saw a lone sheep at the top of the hill that had not joined the group moving toward the bottom. She simply shouted, "Look back, Tan. LOOK BACK!" The dog went right back to the top, found the stray and brought it down with the others.

Incidentally, 99% of all border collies are black with white markings. Light brown coloring, as Tan has, is found only in about 1 in 100.

Angela starts the homeward ride down the hill with Moss leading the way.

Her work completed for the moment, Moss amuses herself by exploring a rabbit hole. Legend has it that the game of golf was invented in Scotland hundreds of years ago with just such a rabbit hole playing an essential role. A lonely shepherd tending his sheep was swinging his crook at stones on the ground when, quite by accident, he dropped one into a rabbit hole. Little did he know the future madness he would create when he mumbled, "I wonder if I can do that again."

SHEEP FEEDING IN LATE AFTERNOON
Near Dunscore
Dumfries and Galloway Region

Epilogue

With the background symphony of waves gently lapping at the shore, I sat staring dreamily at the North Sea from the rocky beach at Inverbervie on the Grampian coast south of Aberdeen. My subconscious thoughts drifted in disarrayed patterns with the ebb and flow of the tides. I had been to this beach many times before, but now, on a cold November afternoon, I was seeing things I had not noticed before. Tomorrow I would be leaving Scotland, not knowing when or if I'd ever be back. My enlistment in the Marine Corps was ending. My plans for the future were uncertain. The distant horizon, which never seemed to get any closer, greatly contributed to a feeling of smallness, of insignificance, of inadequacies. The generally overwhelming vastness surrounding me was certainly conducive to the thoughts in my head bouncing around looking for fertile ground to take root and develop. I wonderingly mused the consequences.

So it was that I began to think, while noticing the beach covered with millions of smooth stones. The relentless pounding of the surf creates these smooth stones which, when studied philosophically, offer to us a valuable life lesson. Being that day in one of my contemplative moods, I sat quietly listening to the waves, generally absorbing all the wonderful sights, sounds and smells of Nature around me. I was fascinated with the stones, all perfectly smooth, each with different colors or markings, and in all sizes. Not one had a jagged edge. It was as if they were tossed in a giant tumbler until every rough edge had been worn down. I wondered how many thousands and thousands of years they had been tossed about by the North Sea's fury. In accepting the power greater than themselves, not resisting the changes but in "going with the flow," their rough exteriors had been shaped into works of beauty. People could do well to structure their lives by the lesson offered on the rocky beach at Inverbervie. Our rough exteriors can be made smooth, too. Some opportunities only appear once. Be patient, but be ready.

Glossary

It has been said that we are two countries separated by a common language.
Here are a few terms found in this book that may not be familiar to all readers.

Bairn	— child	Nae	— no
Bap	— soft bread roll	OAP	— Old Age Pensioner, senior citizen
Ben	— mountain	Pram	— baby carriage or stroller
Cairn	— heap of stones piled up as a memorial or landmark	RAF	— Royal Air Force
Firth	— an arm of a sea where a river empties into it	Reiver	— raider, thief
Fortnight	— period of two weeks, contraction of fourteen nights	Shilling	— old British monetary unit, now equal to five pence
Gaelic	— ancient language of Scotland, now spoken primarily in the Outer Hebrides and remote parts of the Highlands	Single-track — one lane road with widened pullouts for passing	
Glen	— valley	Slainte	— Gaelic word for "to your health" or "cheers"
Jumper	— sweater	Slurry	— liquefied manure used as fertilizer
Kirk	— church	WC	— water closet, toilet
Loch	— lake	Wee	— small
Lorry	— delivery truck	Western Isles — Outer Hebrides, group of islands off the west coast of Scotland	
Moor	— open expanse of boggy wasteland		

SNOWY MARCH MORNING
Near Morebattle
Borders Region

From the lone shieling of the misty island
mountains divide us and the waste of seas —
Yet still the blood is strong, the heart is Highland
And we in dreams behold the Hebrides!
Fair these broad meads; these hoary woods are grand;
But we are exiles from our father's land.

CANADIAN BOAT SONG OF DISPUTED AUTHORSHIP